WHY PRAYERS ARE UNANSWERED

WHY PRAYERS ARE UNANSWERED

-and what you can do about it-

JOHN ALLAN LAVENDER

Tyndale House
Publishers, Inc.
Wheaton, Illinois

Library of Congress
Catalog Number 80-65290
ISBN 0-8423-8236-4,
paper
Copyright ©1967, 1980
by John Allan Lavender
All rights reserved.

First Printing, June 1980
Printed in the United
States of America.

*To God's Errand Boy
1886—1966*

A man who wasn't much as most men measure things, but achieved greatness where it really counts—in the eyes of God. A man who, with two years of formal education, barely able to read and write, set out to do what he could for Christ and discovered there is no limit to what God can do through even a simple man when he has all of him. A man who with an unsophisticated singleness of purpose loved more men into the kingdom of God than just about anyone I know. A man who prayed as if chatting with a dear and lifelong friend, reflecting in his total person the serenity and power which prayer alone can provide. A man whose childlike faith and downright goodness were an inspiration to all who knew him—my father.

CONTENTS

Foreword 9

Preface 11

1 *Circuit-Breakers* 17

2 *What It Means to Ask Wrongly* 31

3 *Putting the Brakes on God's Power* 45

4 *When No Is Really Yes* 57

5 *The Answer God Gives* 71

Notes 84

FOREWORD
A Personal Word

The spiritual insights of Dr. John Allan Lavender are penetrating and sound. Moreover, he has the rare ability to explain and communicate God's truth so clearly and attractively that any reader can understand. A likable and inspiring person, John Lavender knows how to help people, and this book deals with matters that are vital to the good and happy life. Personally, I found great value in reading his manuscript and commend this book most enthusiastically to all who need and search for God's help in their own problems.

Dr. Lavender deals with questions that are always being asked concerning prayer and faith, and his answers are clear, cogent, and satisfying. He is versed in the thinking of our day, but more importantly, having experienced God's grace, he is so very competent in leading others to a deep spiritual experience in which perplexity gives way to certainty.

You will be grateful for this book, as I am.

NORMAN VINCENT PEALE

PREFACE
Misuse or Disuse?

A flippant response to the question of why many of our prayers are unanswered might be: "Because we don't pray!" James, the New Testament writer, makes the terse observation:

> *You do not have, because you do not ask.*
> James 4:2

Jesus dulled the barb a bit, but emphasized the same idea. He said:

> *Hitherto you have asked nothing in my name; ask, and you will receive, that your joy may be full.* John 16:24

Ponder these words and you may agree. Perhaps prayer is a farce instead of a force in your life for the simple reason that you do not use it. You may be speaking *of* God but not *to* him. Like many others, your prayer life may be suffering as much from *dis*use as *mis*use.

To leave the problem there, however, would be unfair. Behind any hesitancy to pray now may be past unsuccessful attempts which have conditioned you to feel "there's no use praying because it won't work anyway." It is to this attitude, and those who hold it, that this volume is directed. I do not claim to know all the answers. In fact, I'm sure I don't even know some of the questions! Nevertheless I have tried to dissect the anatomy of prayer, diagnose the more common ailments, and prescribe from the available spiritual pharmacopeia some correctives which can help you make this greatest of all powers "work."

I owe a significant debt to several authors and commentators whose insight into prayer has helped me crystallize my own thinking. Prominent among these are W.E. Borne (whose provocative sermon on this subject started my creative juices flowing), S.D. Gordon (*Quiet Talks on Prayer*, New York: Fleming H. Revell Co., 1904), Herbert Booth Smith (*Science and Prayer*, New York: Fleming H. Revell Co., 1924), and Donald J. Campbell (*The Adventure of Prayer*, Nashville: Abingdon Press, 1949).

I also am indebted to the most wonderful personal secretary any pastor ever had, Mrs. Grant Marshall. Without Margie's tireless help in typing and correcting the manuscript, plus her quiet goading to get it done, I fear this book might still be a babe unborn. I want to thank Kathy Souer for her editorial assistance. I also want to express gratitude to the good people of the First Baptist Church of Bakersfield, California, whose gracious and eager acceptance of my pulpit offerings has challenged the best that is in me. To Dr. Norman Vincent Peale goes a special word of appreciation for his encouragement and guidance.

God knows our needs before we ask. Then, what is prayer for? Not to inform him, nor to move him, unwilling, to have mercy, as if like some proud prince he requires a certain amount of recognition of his greatness as the price of his favors. Prayer fits our own hearts by conscious need, true desire, and dependence to receive the gifts which he is ever willing to give, but which we are not always fit to receive. As St. Augustine has phrased it: the empty vessel is by prayer carried to the full fountain.

ALEXANDER MACLAREN

ONE
Circuit-Breakers

It is easy to have faith when you are sick and ask for healing, and it comes. It is not difficult to believe in prayer when you are caught up in trouble and plead for guidance, and you receive it. Anyone can trust in God when, having petitioned heaven for the protection of a loved one, he sees that one come through unscathed.

But when you ask for healing and it does not come; when you pray for guidance and you do not get it; when you plead some cause and the heavens seem as brass, *then* it is not so easy to have faith. Then it is a bit more difficult to believe in the power of prayer. In fact, the temptation is to say, as one man said to me quite candidly, "John, I've quit praying. God obviously isn't listening."

His experience is not an isolated one. Perhaps you have prayed and had no answer. Perhaps you have decided not to pray anymore. You may have concluded that prayer, while apparently useful to others, has no value for you. It is possible you do not know what to think. You want to believe. You want to be a person of faith. You want to hurl yourself on the mercies of God with utter abandon, but you are haunted by a lurking fear that it just won't work . . . that your prayers will not be heard . . . that God will let you down. Because you fear the fragile bit of faith you do possess will die if dampened by further disappointment, leaving you with no faith at all, you have carefully tucked it under glass where it can be seen but not touched, admired but not tested. And you struggle on alone.

What a pity! The law of life is that we lose what we do not use, while that which we stretch grows strong. If you expose your faith to testing, it will toughen. If you exert it, it will come alive. And, through this exercise of faith, prayer will become the force you want it to be instead of the farce it may have been.

If you are going to cooperate as much as possible with God in your prayer life, you must be sensitively aware of twelve ailments pointed out in Scripture which put that relationship in jeopardy. These sort themselves into two basic categories: those things which completely thwart your prayers by cutting off God's power and those which reduce the effectiveness of your prayers by placing limitations on God.

I call the first category "spiritual circuit-breakers." These are those ailments which sever the lines of communication between yourself and the heavenly Father so that for all practical purposes your prayers cannot "get through."

Ailment One: A SENSE OF UNCONFESSED SIN

If I had cherished iniquity in my heart, the Lord would not have listened. Psalm 66:18

Please note the verse does not say you must be sinless to be heard. The weight of that word "cherish" is to "fondle," "tolerate," or "foster" sin. Moral and spiritual perfection are not prerequisites to power in prayer. If they were, no one could pray effectively. There is too much sin in the best of us. Furthermore, our worst failings are often unknown to us; they are exposed only as we draw close to Christ.

But when you are made aware of your sin and do nothing about it, when you have a sense of failing and refuse to confess it to God, then this sense of unconfessed sin acts like a circuit-breaker. It disconnects you from the Source of power. And, though God wants to help you, he can't. You won't let him!

Isaiah makes this clear in chapter 59 of his great book:

Behold, the Lord's hand is not shortened, that it cannot save, or his ear dull, that it cannot hear; but your iniquities have made a separation between you and your God. Isaiah 59:1, 2

The problem, you see, is not topside. It is inside.

1 Peter 3:7 applies this truth to a Christian husband who desires to see his unsaved wife converted, or who hopes to woo a Christian

wife who has "carnaled out" back into fellowship with Christ.

> *Likewise you husbands, live considerately with your wives, bestowing honor on the woman as the weaker sex, since you are joint heirs of the grace of life, in order that your prayers may not be hindered.*

His first and foremost concern should be *his* behavior, not hers. His relationship to Jesus, not hers. His concept of the servant's heart, not hers.

Hence a principle emerges: The first thing that should concern you in your conversation with God is personal cleansing. Before you pray for a change in circumstances, you should pray for a change in character. When you do—when you actually confess your sin—he is faithful and just, and will forgive those sins and cleanse us from all unrighteousness (1 John 1:9). In that moment of God-washed cleanness, new boldness and effectiveness in prayer will follow. God says so!

> *The prayer of a righteous man [that is, a man made right by the cleansing action of God's grace] has great power in its effects.* James 5:16

You may fail God again the same day. In fact, you may fail him before you are through praying. One of the most shattering discoveries of my own prayer life has been the fact that in the very midst of my conversation with God I can cut off communication by any one of a dozen different infantile or sub-Christian emotions and thoughts. You may have experienced this problem too. But when the Holy Spirit waves the flag of warning, when you realize you are out of tune and the lines of communication are in jeopardy again, you can stop where you are and as you are and can say: "Father, I was wrong just then. I was way off base. Forgive me. Help me to be right."

You may be thinking: "That's all well and good, but you don't understand. It wouldn't be so bad if I failed God and asked for forgiveness and then failed him again. My problem is that I ask forgiveness and fail him again and again and again and again! I find myself doing the same things over and over and over until I just haven't the gall to ask God to forgive me any more. I feel I'm not worthy of his help."

Of course, you aren't. You never were. Who *is* ever worthy of what the heavenly Father has done and still wants to do? It is not a matter of being worthy. It is a matter of being willing — willing to let God be what he wants to be: a very present help in trouble.

Many sensitive people are harder on themselves than God is. They are not ready to live with the fact of their humanness. But the Bible says:

He [God] knows our frame; he remembers that we are dust. Psalm 103:14

God knows the stuff of which you are made. He knows the ease with which you slip into temptation. Therefore he has gone out of his way to make help available when you need it — to provide forgiveness when you fall. Don't think that asking for forgiveness is a matter of gall. It is a matter of God's boundless and all-sufficient grace. The wonderful good news of the gospel is this:

> *[The Son] In whom we have redemption, the forgiveness of sins.* Colossians 1:14

This news means there is nowhere you can go, there is nothing you can do, there is no pathway of sin into which you can wander, that will place you outside the boundaries of God's all-sufficient grace. Forgiveness is always available, if you want it.

A widow from the slums of New York was invited by a kindly benefactor to spend the weekend at an oceanside cottage. This woman had enjoyed few luxuries. In fact, she often was happy to have just the necessities of life. As she stood by the surging sea that afternoon, overwhelmed by the vast expanse of water, a tear slipped out of the corner of her eye and meandered down her cheek. When her friend asked why she was crying, she replied, "Because it's so wonderful to see something there is enough of."

Well, there is enough of God's grace for you. There is enough of God's love for you. There is enough of God's pardon for you. There is enough of God's power for you. And, if you will receive it, "the sin that doth so easily beset you" will be removed by the sometimes caustic but always cleansing agent of confession. And *your* prayers — when they are the fervent effectual prayers of a person made right by the boundless grace of God — will be characterized by power.

Norman Vincent Peale tells a boyhood incident. He got hold of a big, black cigar, headed into a back alley where no one would see him, and lit it. It didn't taste good, but it made him feel very grown up until he saw his father coming. Norman quickly put the cigar behind his back and tried to be as casual as possible. They exchanged pleasantries for a moment. Then, trying to divert his father's attention in any way possible, Norman spied a billboard advertising the circus.

"Can I go, Dad?" he pleaded. "Can I go to the circus when it comes to town? Please, Dad?"

His father's reply was one Norman never forgot. It is one we ought to remember too.

"Son," he answered quietly but firmly, "one of the first lessons you need to learn about life is this: Never make a petition while at the same time trying to hide a smoldering disobedience behind your back."[1]

It is not God who stops your prayer. His arm is not shortened. His ear is not dull. It is your sin that has gotten in the way! And, if you want to have communion with him, you must cleanse your heart of the smoldering disobediences you are trying to hide. You must not cherish (that is, you must not fondle or nurture) sin in your heart. A sense of unconfessed sin is a hindrance to prayer.

Ailment Two: AN UNFORGIVING SPIRIT

Alongside a sense of unconfessed sin you can place the second spiritual circuit-breaker — an unforgiving spirit.

Art Linkletter has a book entitled *Kids Say the Darndest Things*. And they do! A little boy who had not gone to Sunday school very often was asked by his parents to say a prayer as he went to bed. The youngster formed a prayer based on what he thought he had heard in Sunday school. It came out like this: "Father, forgive us our trash baskets, as we forgive those who put their trash in our baskets!"

You may smile at the little boy's slip, but when it comes down to the heart of the matter, he wasn't far off. Folks *do* go around putting trash in your basket. They say the darndest things — just as kids do — but they are meaner and more vicious. Even so, you cannot hold bitterness in your heart. You have to forgive them even though they may not want to be forgiven. If you don't, the heat in your heart will activate that second spiritual circuit-breaker, the power of your prayers will be instantly cut off, and you will be plunged into personal darkness again.

It is easier to talk about forgiving than it is to forgive. Perhaps the hardest thing about forgiveness is that you often find yourself having to forgive over and over again. It seems as if the same people keep putting their trash in your basket! But there is a great principle which applies here, one which I have already mentioned. It is the gracious forgiveness of God, forgiveness so all-sufficient that no matter how often you sin against him—even in the same way, on the same day—it still applies. His forgiveness toward us is boundless, and so must ours be toward others.

Have you ever noticed how often Jesus put forgiveness and prayer together? If you want the surprise of your life, read the Gospels and see how often and in how many ways Jesus coupled these two. The forgiveness he talks about is not only that which you should desire for yourself. It is the forgiveness you should also be prepared to focus on others.

Do you recall the incident recorded in the eighteenth chapter of Matthew in which Jesus is talking alone with the disciples? Peter remembers the many references Jesus has made to prayer and forgiveness going together. Based on these, he makes his contribution to the conversation.

"Lord," he asks, "how often should I forgive my brother when he fails me? Seven times?"

How very much like Peter! So boisterous and impetuous, so full of the wrong kind of pride, so sure he has arrived spiritually! He is willing to forgive seven times—more than double the three times required by Hebrew law! But the Lord smiles at Peter's immaturity, even as he must smile at ours. "Peter," he answers, "forgiveness is not a limited thing. You are not to forgive seven times. You are to forgive seventy times seven."

Seventy times seven comes to four hundred ninety. You are to forgive others four hundred ninety times—for the same thing! More, if necessary! Jesus was trying to teach Peter (and you) that forgiveness is not a matter of mathematics. It is not a matter of keeping tabs on people. It is not an act but an attitude, not a spurt but a spirit.

One can almost see the Master as he focuses those penetrating eyes on Peter, hoping the disciple will get the point — hoping he will stop counting, or maybe lose count, when people put their trash in his basket. He is hoping Peter will forgive them without limit — that he will react to them with a love that is not weak but meek, a love that does not tire of being gracious, a love that starts forgiving and gets the habit.

Not only is the heart made right by this attitude; it is also made light. Having extended forgiveness to others, you are more ready to receive it yourself. Somehow you sense that the lines of communication have been restored. Now you can ask what you will, confident you will be heard.

Ailment Three: AN UNSURRENDERED WILL

A third circuit-breaker is an unsurrendered will:

You ask and do not receive, because you ask wrongly. . . . James 4:3

Succeeding pages will deal more fully with what it means to "ask wrongly," but in the context of our present discussion, this expression means to pray with the wrong motive or purpose: that is, to ask for the right thing for the wrong reason. For instance, you may pray that your husband might become a Christian, but only because life would be so much easier for you if he weren't so belligerent and hateful. You may pray for the guidance of your daughter, but only so that you won't have to toss around in bed wondering where she is when she stays out a little late. You may pray for a better and more challenging job, but only to get a larger income and buy more and more of the things you need less and less. The prayers themselves are not necessarily wrong. The problem is the motive—the purpose behind them. It is a wonderful thing to pray for the conversion of a husband, or for the will of God for your children, or for more challenging work. But God cannot honor a selfish motive. If he did, he would destroy character.

When your children come to you with selfish petitions, you are not likely to grant these. You want to build their character. You want your children to know they cannot surrender to every selfish whim which strikes their fancy. God does not want you to become a character-weakling either. So, whenever an unsurrendered will is expressed in a false motive, the circuit-breaker goes into action. The power is cut off. The prayer does not "get through."

In intercessory prayer the problem is multiplied, for here not only your will is involved but that of the person for whom you are praying. (In praying for some great cause like world peace the wills of millions of people enter the picture.) Even though your will is fully yielded to God's desire *that all should reach repentance* (2 Peter 3:9), an unsurrendered will on the part of the person (or persons) for whom you are praying can neutralize your prayer and cause it to go unanswered.

This fact is terribly frustrating, especially if you are interceding for a loved one such as a child or spouse. But in no other situation are you so apt to draw so near to the heart of God. He, too, pauses before the royalty of human will. Wisely and lovingly, he elects not to violate it. A poet has said:

> In many ways He will be good and kind
> But God will never force the human mind.

Here is a mystery of major magnitude. However, it remains a fact. The only thing capable of thwarting God's willingness to bless is man's unwillingness to be blessed.

This is not to say you should cease praying for this person. God's time and way do not always coincide with your own (Isaiah 55:8, 9). Nor do we sufficiently understand the *modus operandi* of intercessory prayer to say with precision how heavily perseverance weighs in obtaining an answer, but it cannot be lightly dismissed.

Having acknowledged the complications that can arise when praying for others, do not forget the role your own will plays in personal prayer.

Penetrate the meaning of this sentence: "This I ask in Jesus' name, Amen." You may have said these words many times. But have you ever stopped to realize what they mean? To pray something "in Jesus' name" is to say, "I want Jesus to sponsor this prayer. I want him to stand up and speak for it—to put his weight behind it." But if that is what you are asking, you must be certain your petition is compatible with his life and example.

To pray "in Jesus' name" is to say in substance, "Lord, this is how it looks to me. From my limited point of view I think it ought to come out this way. But I do not know everything. If part of my prayer is wrong, then hear and answer only that part of it which is right — that part which is in keeping with your spirit and your name. To pray "in Jesus' name" is to pray with one eye open. It is to keep one eye focused on your prayer itself — examining it, measuring it, weighing it to make certain what you ask is in keeping with the character of the One in whose name you ask it. To pray "in Jesus' name" is to stop giving orders. It is to turn command and authority over to him. It is to accept the simple fact that the purpose of prayer is not to change life to suit you, but to change you to suit life.

CORRECTIVES

For Ailment One
A Sense of Unconfessed Sin. Good news: Forgiveness is possible! The thoughts, words, deeds, and feelings which have raised havoc with your prayer life can be removed by the often caustic but always cleansing agent of confession (1 John 1:9). When you are clean clear through, *your* prayers — the effectual, fervent prayers of a person made right by the goodness of God — will be characterized by power.

For Ailment Two
An Unforgiving Spirit. Search to see if the heat of hate or hostility has activated a circuit-breaker

and cut off the power. If so, restore the connection by praying: "Renew a right spirit within me." Pray these words often. Learn to forgive as you have been forgiven — boundlessly.

For Ailment Three
An Unsurrendered Will. If God is saying "no" to you, it may be that somewhere, somehow, you (or those for whom you pray) are saying "no" to him. Stop giving orders. Let God take command. Do not fear his will. Seek it. It is your highest good. Pray for wisdom that you may be in his will, that you may not block his way.

TWO
What It Means to Ask Wrongly

One day when Julie, our youngest, was three years old, she created quite a ruckus when I refused to let her have her mother's brand new dagger-like sewing scissors to play with. Later that evening, Jeff, then nine, felt sure I didn't love him because I rejected his tearful plea for a hot fudge sundae less than two hours after he had eaten a full-course dinner topped off with pie and ice cream. On other occasions, Jodi, our firstborn, has felt abused because her daddy turned a deaf ear to requests that were just as dangerous and unhealthy. In each case my children thought I was an old meany who did not love them. But if they had looked at their request through other eyes, they would have known that my denial, instead of being evidence of my indifference, was proof positive of my love.

Now, if your prayer experience is at all typical,

it is shot through with requests which God apparently has not heard. You have come to him with your urgent pleas and plaintive petitions, but the desired response has not come. As a result you have been tempted to think God does not care or is not listening. Wrong on both counts! There is a difference between prayers that are unheard and prayers that are unanswered. God has promised to hear all petitions of those who come to him with a clean heart and a right spirit. He has said concerning man:

And if he cries to me, I will hear, for I am compassionate. Exodus 22:27

But, while God promises to hear all prayers, he nowhere promises to satisfy all whims. He will not make himself a cosmic bellhop who delivers what you want—where and when you want it.

Actually, the Bible is full of illustrations of unanswered prayer. There was Moses who prayed that he might enter the Promised Land, but who died on Nebo's lonely mountain. There was the Psalmist who prayed around the clock on one occasion without an answer. And, in a moment of despair he cried:

O my God, I cry by day, but thou dost not answer; and by night, but find no rest. Psalm 22:2

And there was the prophet, who voiced the anguished exclamation:

Thou hast wrapped thyself with a cloud so that no prayer can pass through. Lamentations 3:44

There was also Paul, who besought his Lord three times for relief from a thorn in the flesh without success. There was Jesus himself, who in the garden prayed that he might be spared exposure to the malignancy of man's sin, but his prayer was not answered. Some of history's greatest persons have had to learn the patience of unanswered prayer.

Nevertheless, while those prayers were unanswered, we cannot say they were unheard. On the contrary, those prayers were heard in precisely the same way Julie's request for a pair of scissors and Jeff's request for a hot fudge sundae were heard. I was not indifferent to my children's pleas. If there had been any way of granting their request without damage to their well-being, I would gladly have done so. I love them. But I would not have been kind to my little girl had I provided her with a spear-like instrument with which she might have seriously and permanently injured herself. I would not have done my son a favor if I had allowed him to indulge excessively in sweets which could have undermined his health. Nor should you accuse God of being deaf or indifferent because he is wise! He sees what you cannot see. He knows what you do not know. Therefore, his judgment is far better than your own.

Put this down as a profound but simple truth: "God's will is your highest good." When you pray and your prayer is unanswered, the reason is not that God is deaf or indifferent. It is that he knows *now* what, in time, you *will* know. His plan for you is better than anything you can plan for yourself.

The Book of James, which tells more about prayer than any other book in the Bible, contains these words of wisdom:

> *You ask, and do not receive, because you ask wrongly.* James 4:3

In other words, when you pray without apparent success, your disappointment may not be caused by any of the circuit-breakers mentioned in Chapter 1 but by some fault in the character of your prayer itself. You "ask and do not receive" because you ask in the wrong way or for the wrong things.

Ailment Four: A DISREGARD FOR NATURAL LAW
It may be that your prayer has been ineffective because you have prayed without regard for the natural order of things. I am thinking right now of a schoolboy who prayed God would make San Francisco the state capital of California because that is what he wrote on his examination paper. He knew the correct answer began with S and ended with O, but could not remember what went in between. So, hoping for an "A" on his paper, he earnestly prayed God would make his wild guess the right answer.

"Obviously God couldn't answer a prayer like

that," you reason. "Think of the chaos involved if the Capitol building were suddenly airlifted from Sacramento to the city by the Golden Gate." Perhaps so. But a little boy became disillusioned with prayer because God failed to change the capital of California to accommodate him.

A college student also gave up praying because he had not received the scholarship for which he had prayed so hard and worked so long. He forgot that for every scholarship there were a dozen potential winners who had prayed and worked equally as hard as he. Even an omnipotent God could award the limited number of scholarships to only a small percentage of the applicants. You see, there is a natural order to things and you are guilty of praying wrongly when you pray without regard for natural law.

From the point of view of religion, there are two possible attitudes to take toward natural law. One of these is that God has made this a universe of law and, being law-abiding, has made himself subject to his own laws. This interpretation gives you a kind of captive God — a God who might want to suspend these laws under certain conditions, but cannot do so now that he has set them in operation. This view explains many instances of unanswered prayer, particularly those relating to accidental situations.

A few years ago I had a convertible which I enjoyed very much. One lovely summer day I was driving along with the top down when I heard a mother yell, "Tommy, come back here!"

Instinctively I slammed my foot on the brake and came to a halt. Out of the corner of my eye I saw a little boy, about four years of age, dart across the street in front of me, directly into the path of an oncoming car whose driver had not yet seen him. Realizing the danger, I blew my horn and prayed: "Oh God, don't let it happen."

Almost simultaneously, the mother began to scream, "No, God, no!" Apparently my horn and the screams attracted the attention of the other driver, for she hit her brakes. The expression of horror I saw on her face verified for me her later testimony that when she saw the child and applied her brakes, she prayed, "God, don't let me hit him." But, in spite of her prayer, she did hit him.

Now, from the point of view of the first interpretation of natural law, you would have to say that even though God wanted very much to spare Tommy the pain of serious injury, he was powerless to do so because he had made himself a captive of his own laws. There were forces at work in that moment which he could not conveniently suspend. To do so would result in havoc. And, while this particular point of view answers certain questions about unanswered prayer, in the judgment of many it is inadequate.

There is a second interpretation. This is the view that natural law is something which having been created by God is now sustained by him day in and day out, moment by moment, eon after eon, because in his loving wisdom he knows this is best.

Actually, what science calls natural law is

really nothing more than the sum total of man's observations on how things work. The scientist has observed that under certain conditions, certain things behave in a certain way—every single time. And, because they always have acted in this way, he is led to the erroneous conclusion that they *must* do so, whether God wants them to or not. A more meaningful and to my way of thinking more accurate conclusion is this: The predictable behavior which science observes and calls natural law is really the love, wisdom, and faithfulness of God at work.

Natural law operates with dependability because God wants it that way. Thus, G.K. Chesterton's earthy comment that the sun doesn't rise because of natural law but because God says "Get up and do it again" may be closer to the truth than the most precise system of astronomy which omits God.

How does prayer fit into this understanding of the order of things? Well, in the first place, you must reckon with the fact that it is God's faithfulness in sustaining his laws which makes life possible on this planet. Suppose the chemical ingredients of your food were the product of caprice. Suppose there were no dependability about it. Suppose the food you eat today and find nourishing turned out to be poisonous tomorrow. You would be in a terrible fix. It would become necessary that every nutrient you now enjoy be subjected to exhaustive tests each time it was used, lest on some occasion it would prove harmful to you. Or suppose the various laws governing gravitation, propulsion, momentum, or the endless physical laws you have come to count on, were subject to the sudden and arbitrary whims of a changeable mind. Not only would life be destroyed on this planet, but the planet itself would be put in jeopardy. You can live and move and have your being—you can plan with some sense of security about the future—because, and only because, this is a universe of law. And since you wish to live and move and have your being—since you wish to be able to plan your future with some sense of security—you should also want God to continue to sustain his laws, because this is the best for you and for all mankind.

This confidence in the ultimate good of an orderly universe should be your conviction in spite of the fact that the same laws which sustain life are capable of destroying it. Earthquakes, fires, floods, sickness, even death are part of the natural order of things. And when, in spite of all your praying, someone you love and desperately need is taken from you as a result of some catastrophe, the insights of Christian faith should lead you to say: God did not will this individual tragedy, but he did will the laws and the continuation of those laws which permitted it.

Does that outlook on life seem bad? Look at the case of little Tommy again. At least three people prayed he would not be hurt. I prayed. His mother prayed. The driver of the other car prayed. But we were praying wrongly. The sparing of his injury was incompatible with natural order. The scientific principle known as inertia made it impossible to stop the car in the short distance remaining, and if God had suspended that principle once, the movement of objects such as automobiles would never again have been dependable. And if the car was allowed to strike the child (as it was), the only way for him not to be hurt would be for all the warm, soft, human characteristics which made him a lovable child to suddenly change into some kind of impervious material which could resist the shock of being hit by a ton of steel going twenty miles an hour. If such a change could occur, all the natural laws operating at that moment would become equally subject to suspension. Nothing would be dependable, and unimaginable misery would thereby be inflicted on the other four billion inhabitants of the earth. At that moment the sparing of this little boy's injury was imcompatible with the continuance of natural law. Therefore, God chose the greater good. God allowed the tragedy to happen not because he is unloving or indifferent to the pain of a little boy, but because he is truly loving, because he is sensitive to the chaos which a capricious act — however well intentioned — could inflict upon the whole human race.

To pray, therefore, without regard for the natural order of things — whether it be for San Francisco to become the capital of California or for the laws of physics to be suspended — is to pray wrongly. You should not rebuke God as being unfeeling or unwise when such prayers are unanswered. Rather, seek to understand the true love and wisdom which are characteristic of his way.

Ailment Five: A DISREGARD FOR OTHERS

A second manner in which you may be guilty of praying wrongly is when you pray without regard for the welfare of others. This ailment is not unrelated to my previous point. While God sees the individual, he also sees the crowd. He will not do anything to benefit one person that would be to the detriment of many.

> *The Lord looks down from heaven, he sees all the sons of men.* Psalm 33:13.

Suppose, for instance, I am scheduled to give an address in Oakland, four hundred miles north of Bakersfield, California, where I live. Arrangements are made for a flight which will take me directly to that city. But, because of carelessness on my part, I miss the plane. Feverishly I check with the airlines and discover there is another flight destined for San Francisco, across the bay from Oakland. The passenger agent estimates that if the flight is on time and if I can secure an adventurous taxicab driver who will take me across the Bay Bridge at breakneck speed, I just might make my speaking engagement. So I climb aboard the plane, praying all the while that by some sort of miracle I will avoid the embarrassment of missing an engagement resulting from my carelessness. Lo and behold, as the plane approaches the airport, the pilot announces over the intercom that due to heavy fog over San

Francisco we will land in Oakland. Absolutely thrilled at the miraculous way God has answered my prayers, I deplane in Oakland and grab a taxi which speeds me to my speaking engagement in good time.

However, while my convenience is being served, there is a doctor on the plane who is desperately needed at a San Francisco hospital for emergency surgery. Because of this delay his patient has been put in jeopardy. Another public speaker, scheduled to make a much more important address than I, has been placed under great strain by this "miracle" which has taken place for my own private benefit and, after a wild taxi trip through heavy traffic, arrives at his meeting just in the nick of time. The poor chairman of that particular program nearly has ulcers because his star attraction is late. And the other passengers are subjected to varying degrees of anxiety, as are the crew members whose plans have been upset. All of this distress has occurred so that I, who had missed an earlier flight due to carelessness, might be spared the embarrassment of arriving late for a speaking engagement.

Obviously I have overstated the case for emphasis. But surely you can see the chaos that would result if God indiscriminately answered individual prayers without concern for the total good. Therefore, if at times you pray in blind or selfish disregard for the needs and rights of others, you may expect your prayers to be unanswered. God, who "knoweth and doeth all things well," will not needlessly burden or inconvenience many to accommodate the one.

Ailment Six: A DISREGARD FOR GOD'S SOVEREIGNTY

Finally, you may be guilty of "praying wrongly" when you pray without regard for the sovereignty of God. If all your prayers were answered, you, not God, would be in control of things. You would be the ruler of earth. And, though the thought might be enticing for a moment, I am sure you don't feel you could govern things better than he.

A Scottish woman earned a modest living by peddling her wares along the roads of her country. When she came to an intersection, she would toss a stick into the air to determine which way to go. On one occasion she was seen tossing the stick into the air not once but three times. When asked why, she replied, "Because the first two times it pointed a way I didn't want to go!"

Many of your prayers may be like that. You ask God for guidance, but when on occasion he directs you down a dull or difficult road, you choose another path because it seems brighter. How unfortunate! Though you see only the road's beginning, God sees its ending too. He knows which way is truly best. So do not try to thwart his will. Seek it. Do not pray in such a fashion as to deny his sovereignty. Acknowledge it. Remember: what God plans for you is better than anything you can plan for yourself! Pursue prayer in this conviction, and you will discover it really does change things for the better.

Two little children were playing house. One was a five-year-old, the other three. In the course of their playtime, the mother overheard the older child say, "Now it's time to go to bed. First we must say our prayers."

Kneeling down beside their make-believe bed in their make-believe house, the children folded their hands and bowed their heads. The older one prayed, "We've had a lovely day today, God. What do you plan for Tuesday?"

Those simple words express the kind of faith and trust God wants from you. He loves you. He longs to help and please you. He wants to work with you so all things will fit into a pattern for your good. If you will let him—if you will commit yourself to him in such a way that you do his will as if it were your own—then you will set in motion forces which make it possible for him to do your will as if it were his own. When that happens, the faith-filled words of a little child can become your prayer too: "I've had a lovely day today, God. What do you plan for Tuesday?"

CORRECTIVES

For Ailment Four
A Disregard For Natural Law. To pray without regard for natural law is to pray wrongly. Do not rebuke God as being unfeeling or unwise when such prayers are unanswered. Rather, seek to understand better the true love and wisdom of his way.

For Ailment Five
A Disregard For Others. While God sees the individual, he also sees the crowd. If, therefore, you

pray in blind or selfish disregard for the needs of others, your prayers will be unanswered. God will not bless one to the detriment of many. To enrich your prayers —*and their product* —widen the scope of your concern.

For Ailment Six
A Disregard For God's Sovereignty. God sees what you cannot see. He knows what you cannot know. Do not try to outguess him. Submit to his sovereignty. His plan for you is better than anything you can plan for yourself.

THREE
Putting the Brakes on God's Power

Roland Hayes, the singer, quotes his untutored but sage grandfather as saying the trouble with many prayers is "no suction"! I doubt if the most learned theologian could improve upon that diagnosis, for the picturesque speech of this plain man illuminates still a third set of reasons for unanswered prayers.

Ailment Seven: A LACK OF FAITH

Light on this factor is found in the book of James.

> *If any of you lacks wisdom, let him ask of God... and it will be given him. But let him ask in faith, with no doubting, for he who doubts is like a wave of the sea that is driven and tossed by the wind. For that person must not suppose that [he] will receive anything from the Lord.* James 1:5-7

One of the perennial dreams of the scientific mind has been to harness the restless energy of the sea. If only the power of the breaking waves could be converted into electricity, what fabulous things could be accomplished! Limitless power would be available. Thus far, however, all attempts have met with frustration and failure. The surface of the sea is too undependable. The waves cannot be counted on. One moment they are carried forward by the wind. The next they are driven back. And if your faith is like the waves, says James, if you trust in God, but with reservations, there is little likelihood you will receive much from him.

This principle is in total harmony with the teachings of Jesus. Our Lord repeatedly declared that faith is a basic ingredient in effective prayer:

According to your faith be it done to you. Matthew 9:29

If you have faith as a grain of mustard seed . . . nothing will be impossible to you. Matthew 17:20

Your faith has saved you; go in peace. Luke 7:50

If you have faith, and never doubt . . . it will be done. Matthew 21:21

Five different times the Gospel writers record Jesus as saying:

Your faith has made you well. Matthew 9:22; Mark 5:34, 10:52; Luke 8:48, 17:19

So important is faith that Jesus said to Peter:

I have prayed for you, that your faith may not fail. Luke 22:32

Jesus did not pray that Peter would be good, or brave, or clever, or wise. He prayed that Peter would have a faith which could not fail, which would endure in spite of every adversity.

Now, it is possible your prayers are not answered because you do not expect an answer. You have come to God with your petitions, laying your concerns before him; then, picking them up, you have started worrying again over the very things about which you prayed barely moments before. You do not expect anything to happen as a result of your prayers, and you get exactly what you expect!

Do you remember the story of Peter, who had been tossed into prison? It is found in Acts 12. His fellow Christians in Jerusalem decided to pray for his release. While they were still in prayer, God miraculously delivered him.

With the help of the Bible narrative we can visualize the dramatic events which followed. Peter, elated, ran over to the prayer meeting to offer himself as a personal demonstration of the power of prayer. He knocked on the door, but the people were so busy praying for his release they had no time to answer. He continued rapping until a little girl by the name of Rhoda got up off her knees and tiptoed over to the door to quiet whoever was creating this disturbance. When she saw it was Peter, she became so excited she left him standing outside, ran back to the prayer meeting, and cried, "Stop praying! Peter's here! God has answered us!"

One dour old Christian looked up and said, "Shhh! We are praying."

And her mother added, "Hush, child, don't be silly. This is serious business. Get down on your knees and help us pray for Peter's release."

"But, Mommy," Rhoda replied, "Peter is at the door!"

All the while poor old Peter was rapping his knuckles raw. Finally, in exasperation, the people stopped praying to see who was creating all the disturbance. When they opened the door and saw Peter, they were "astonished." This is the Bible's decorous way of saying they just about fainted!

Now do not judge these people too harshly. It is possible that you too have prayed with the same limited measure of expectancy — not really believing anything would happen. And perhaps you too would be "astonished" if your prayers actually got things done. Because of this lack of faith, you have put a brake on God's power, leaving yourself with many unanswered prayers.

So, if you want to make prayer a force instead of a farce in your life, hunt for the question marks in your heart. When you find them, dig them out by the roots. If, here and there, you find a particularly pesky one that refuses to yield, take a positive approach by praying with another earnest but honest seeker:

I believe; help my unbelief. Mark 9:24

Ailment Eight: A LACK OF PERSISTENCE

A second brake on God's power which limits the effectiveness of your prayers is a lack of persistence. A lot of people pray the way they duck for apples. Their prayers are perfunctory and casual. They lack the staying quality which stubbornly insists upon being heard and persists until an answer is received. Their prayers have "no suction"!

Persistence in prayer does not mean praying loud or long. The duration and decibels of prayer are not signs of its sincerity. An earnest layman had the unfortunate habit of shouting when he prayed in public. After one occasion when his prayer had almost caused the rafters to shake, a little girl leaned over to her father and whispered, "Daddy, do you think if he lived nearer to God he wouldn't have to yell so loud?" A wise observation.

Someone has suggested it is not the geometry of your prayers, how long they are; or the arithmetic of your prayers, how many they are; or the rhetorical expression of your prayers, how beautiful they are; or the logical exposition of your prayers, how argumentative they are (and I might add, or the volume of your prayers, how loud they are); it is a fervency of spirit which gets the job done. God's written word agrees:

The prayer of a righteous man has great power in its effects. James 5:16

The importance of persistence in prayer is repeatedly emphasized in the Bible. A classic illustration is the tenacity of the Israelites who marched around Jericho repeatedly in obedience to God's direction. Five times, ten times, twelve times they circled the mighty rampart, but not even a crack appeared. Still they persisted. On the thirteenth time there was a shout, a trumpet blast, and the walls came tumbling down. Persistence, in keeping with God's promise, was the key. What was true then is true now.

If you need further confirmation, listen to what Jesus himself has said:

Ask, and it will be given you; seek, and you will find; knock, and it will be opened to you. Matthew 7:7

There is a note of insistence in these words. Jesus implies that if you have asked and not received, or sought and not found, you should boldly approach the gate of God's goodness and knock, and keep on knocking until the door swings wide and you actually possess that which God has promised.

"Prayer," said Charles Haddon Spurgeon, "is like a rope on a bell. When tugged, the great bell rings in the ears of God. Some scarcely stir the bell, for they pray so languidly; others give but an occasional pinch at the rope. But he who wins with heaven is the man who grasps the rope boldly and pulls continually with all his might."

This persistence is not aimed at getting God to change his mind. God's mind does not need changing. His will for you is always good. He is always more ready to give than you are to receive. Prayer does not change God's mind. Prayer changes *things* — the things in your life which are out of focus, the things which put a brake on God's power, the things which make it impossible for him to bless you as he wants to.

But more than that, persistence in prayer purifies your longings and clarifies your thinking, so they more closely conform to the spirit of the most perfect prayer of all, that of Jesus before his betrayal:

Nevertheless not my will, but thine, be done.
Luke 22:42

To ask rashly is foolish. To seek selfishly is dangerous. To knock flippantly is audacious. But when in dogged faith you persistently pray that God's will may be your own, the sheer daring of prayer becomes glorious. All God has is yours — exceedingly abundant above all you can ask or think.

Ailment Nine: A LACK OF ACTION

Alongside a lack of faith and a lack of persistence you must also recognize that a lack of action can be a brake upon God's power.

A college dean tells of attending a boxing match with a friend who is a Catholic priest. As the fighters entered the ring, one of them crossed himself. The dean turned to the priest and asked, "Father, will that help?"

"It will if he can fight!" the priest replied.

Prayer is no substitute for work. And one reason God may not answer some of your prayers is that he wants *you* to answer them. There is no sense in begging God for that which you can make possible under your own power. Florence Nightingale, that remarkable woman who was years ahead of her time in many ways, emphasized this thought in a question:

> What is the use of praying to be delivered from "plague and pestilence" [the prayer book phrase] so long as the common sewers are allowed to flow into the Thames? If God sends a visitation of cholera, which is the more preferable reading of His mind—that He sends it in order that men might pray to Him for relief from it, or in order that they should themselves be driven to remove the predisposing causes?

The answer is obvious. More than that, it is thoroughly Christian. And what can be said about a dread epidemic can also be said of the other evils making this world sick: war, lust, alcoholism, slums, economic injustice, and the like.

There comes a time when you must stop praying and start working. If your prayers are genuine—more than pious platitudes and timeworn shibboleths—then, having prayed in church on Sunday, you should go out from church to do on Monday what you can to help God answer those prayers.

Ponder the insights that have come to James through the Holy Spirit:

> *What does it profit, my brethren, if a man says he has faith but has not works? Can his faith save him? If a brother or sister is ill-clad and in lack of daily food, and one of you says to them, "Go in peace, be warmed and filled," without giving them the things needed for the body, what does it profit?* James 2:14-16

Christianity is much more than "pie in the sky by and by." It is both a personal *and practical* relationship with God. It is related to the individual and social needs of *now*. As James points out, a man who is hungry is not looking for prayers or a pat on the back. He needs something to eat. It is an affrontery to pray, "Lord, take care of this brother," when you have food you might give him. There is no such thing as a prayer in which you have nothing to do. If you do nothing, you are not praying! The moment comes when to remain on your knees is an insult to God. What is needed is to get up and get going.

Such was God's instruction to the Israelites when in their flight from Egypt they came to the Red Sea. The water was in front of them. The Egyptian army was behind them. They did not know what to do. So Moses drew apart to pray. Do you know what God said to him? "Why do you stand here talking to me? Don't talk to me. Talk to the people. Tell them to go forward!" The time for praying had passed. The time for action had come. Until the Israelites were prepared to act, God was not in a position to fulfill his promise.

Isn't it often the same with you? Time after time you yourself hold the answer to your prayers. In those instances your great need is not faith *and* works, but faith *that* works. If you will work as though everything depends upon you, while praying as though everything depends upon God, you will have the joy and thrill of being part of the answer to your own prayers.

A poor man was injured one day while trying to repair the roof of his modest home. He would be unable to work for quite a while. He had a large family, and on his meager income had been unable to save any money. The future looked grave. Some of his friends decided they should pray for him. The news went out and a group of people met at the church. They presented God with the needs of this man. They prayed that his family might have food and his children might be cared for. In the midst of one particularly pious prayer there came a rapping at the door. Someone got up, walked quietly to the door, opened it, and saw a young farm boy. The lad whispered, "Dad couldn't come to the prayer meeting tonight, so he sent his prayers in a wagon." Down at the curb was a buckboard full of potatoes, beans, canned goods, and fruit.

True prayer always loads its compassion in a wagon. It always puts feet on its petitions and hands on its supplications. It realizes that often a man's best prayer is what he does when he is not praying. It comes eyeball to eyeball with the basic fact that prayer is not a device for getting your will done through God, but a deepdown desire that God's will may be done through you.

CORRECTIVES

For Ailment Seven
A Lack of Faith. Hunt for the question marks in your heart. When you find them, dig them out by the roots. If, here and there, you find a particularly pesky one that refuses to yield, take a positive approach by praying: "I believe you, Lord. Help me to believe you more!"

For Ailment Eight
A Lack of Persistence. If your prayers have "no suction," try tenacity—not to change God's way of thinking, but to clarify your own. Then approach the Throne of Grace with boldness. Knock and keep on knocking till the answer comes.

For Ailment Nine
A Lack of Action. There is no such thing as a prayer in which you have nothing to do. If you do nothing, you are not praying. Put feet on your petitions and hands on your supplications. You hold the answer yourself to many of your prayers. Remember: Your most effective prayers may be what you do when you aren't praying!

FOUR
When No Is Really Yes

God's house of prayer, says Dr. Arthur T. Pierson, is several stories high, and God wants you to explore the entire place. It is sad, therefore, if you limit your visits to the ground floor because it is accessible and a bit more familiar. Some of God's rarest treasures are tucked away in the attic. You will find a more intimate relationship with him only when you mount the stairs of faith.

We can recognize at least four levels in prayer. The first is the ground floor where answers are obvious and immediate. Here is the place to begin. On this plane you are conditioned by experience to attempt the tougher climb to finer things.

It doesn't take much faith to do some things. To push a switch on the wall, for instance, and receive the light this simple act makes possible. You have been conditioned by experience to expect light as a result of completing an electrical circuit. You are disappointed if, on rare occasions, it does not come. Faith is involved here—faith in something outside of, beyond, and above yourself—but it is a rather elementary faith. Nevertheless, having experienced the dependability of electricity's response to your simple gestures of faith, you are encouraged to mount the stairs of learning to more sophisticated electronic concepts.

Similarly you need to begin your exploration of God's house of prayer on the lowest level. Here the results are easy to recognize, like light in response to the flicking of a switch. Through answers which are obvious and immediate, your faith is strengthened. The dependability of God's love is assured. Your spirit is conditioned. You are made ready for the more trying tests to come.

When you attain the second story in God's house of prayer, you discover that some answers are not so easily recognized. Often they are delayed or disguised. A case in point is that of the apostle Paul, who prayed he might go to Rome. When, after long delay, the answer came, it was hardly in the form he had expected. Instead of arriving as a sturdy herald of the triumphant Christ, he was carried in, a victim of shipwreck, barely clinging to a thread of life. His prayer had been answered, but in a way that was delayed and disguised. Only a mature faith, conditioned by long experience, could see the Father's hand, as Paul did.

A still higher plane is the third story in God's

house of prayer where petitions are apparently denied. On the surface the answer is "no." But hindsight reveals the apparent "no" was actually a "yes." More about this in a moment.

The fourth floor is where prayer appears to be entirely unheeded by God. I will deal at length with this in the concluding chapter of this book. But, for the moment, consider: If, on the ground floor, you have experienced obvious and immediate answers to prayer, and if, on that lowest level, you have been repeatedly reminded of the faithfulness of God—that he does indeed work all things together for good—cannot the disappointment of apparently unanswered prayer be left with him? God's time and your time are not the same. He doesn't die as you do. He has all eternity in which to work out his plan. So, in spite of de facto "proof" to the contrary, you must believe God's way is best. The day will dawn when faith gives way to sight and you know in full that which, at the moment, you know only in part. We all look forward to that day.

Having said this much about the highest of prayer planes, I would invite you to return now to the third story—the level on which your literal requests are denied, while your genuine desires are fulfilled. It is here that "no" is really "yes."

Ailment Ten: MISREADING GOD'S KINDNESS

Often God follows this bewildering course out of kindness. He wants to give you more than you asked for. And, as Paul so aptly put it, God is

> *. . .able to do far more abundantly than all that we ask or think . . . .* Ephesians 3:20

Dr. Kenneth N. Taylor is well-known as the paraphraser of *The Living Bible*. Growing out of Dr. Taylor's desire to make the Bible understandable to his ten young children, *The Living Bible* has helped countless people around the world to grasp the vitality and power of God's Word.

Those who are privileged to meet this warm, humble man personally soon discover that Dr. Taylor has great difficulty in speaking. His manner of speech is halting; his voice very hoarse. He sounds much like a man with a severe case of laryngitis. However, his problem is not a temporary one.

During a whirlwind speaking tour for the Moody Literature Mission in 1962, Dr. Taylor caught a lingering cold. Later in the tour while giving a luncheon talk in Portugal, his voice suddenly gave way. At first, it seemed certain Dr. Taylor's problem was nothing more than laryngitis brought on by his cold and the strain of the trip. But months passed and there was no improvement. Doctors were unable to diagnose the difficulty or prescribe effective treatment.

In the ensuing years, Dr. Taylor and his family have prayed repeatedly for a cure, but his condition has not improved.

"My problem is annoying and embarrassing," Dr. Taylor says. "But it has forced me to concentrate on writing and on the publishing company. Without it, I might have been drawn into an extensive number of speaking engagements which would have taken my time and energy away from these other things. God has richly blessed our work here and I am grateful.

"I still hope to be healed, but if God chooses to leave me as I am, I am content."

Instead of spreading the gospel directly through speaking and preaching, Ken Taylor has reached millions with God's truth through *The Living Bible* and other Christian books published by Tyndale House, the publishing company he founded.

The substance of Dr. Taylor's prayer (that he be healed from his vocal difficulties) was denied. But his deeper desire (that he be able to communicate God's truth to others) has been fulfilled. He was given more than he asked for. The "no" was really "yes"!

Ailment Eleven: MISUNDERSTANDING GOD'S WAY

A second reason God takes you to the third level of prayer is to teach you the wisdom of his ways.

> *My thoughts are not your thoughts, neither are your ways my ways, says the Lord. For as the heavens are higher than the earth, so are my ways higher than your ways, and my thoughts than your thoughts.* Isaiah 55:8, 9

The prayers of Monica, the mother of Augustine, for her son are an example. During his formative years Augustine showed little of the saintliness for which he later became famous. In fact, during his youth he was a pleasure-mad cynic. Again and again his devoted mother prayed for his conversion. And, when he announced one day he was going to Rome, a center of sensual living, Monica fervently pleaded with God that he be kept at home.

"If I can't handle him here, Lord," she reasoned, "how can I possibly protect him in that wicked place so far away?"

But, in spite of all her praying, Augustine went to Rome. There, in the course of events, he came under the influence of Ambrose, the great Bishop of Milan, and was converted. Was Monica's prayer answered? Of course! But not in the way she had expected. Her desire that he stay at home was denied. But the desire *behind* her desire (that is, her basic wish that her boy might become a child of God) was granted. The heavenly Father had led her to the third level in his house of prayer so that she might see the ultimate wisdom of his way in working all things together for good.

Ailment Twelve: MISCALCULATING GOD'S PURPOSE

Still a third reason God responds in this strange manner is that some larger purpose might be served. Let me call your attention to the witness of Adoniram Judson, the great Baptist missionary: "I never prayed sincerely and earnestly for anything but it came at sometime — no matter how distant a date — in some shape, probably the last I should have devised, it came."

But look at his life. He asked that he might go to India. He was compelled to go to Burma. He prayed that his beloved wife might be healed. She died and was buried beside their two children for whom he also had prayed. He pleaded with God that he might be released from prison. He lay there for months in chains. How could Adoniram Judson possibly say that his prayers had always been answered?

Think again of the prayer *behind* the prayer. For Judson it was that his life and work as a missionary might have a maximum of meaning to the lives of other men. So when the door to India was closed, God led him to Burma, where he ultimately found fields more white unto harvest than would have been true in the land of his first choosing. When his beloved wife was taken from him, he learned dimensions of human need that enabled him to empathize with the needs of others in a fashion that formerly had been impossible.

There has rarely been a great man who has not known a great sorrow. In drinking deeply from the cup of grief, Adoniram Judson was molded by God into a man who could really minister to the heartaches and heartbreaks of people. When he was kept in prison despite his plea for release, he learned what it meant to be captive.

Thus Christ's description of himself as one who had come to "set the captives free" took on new significance for Judson. Later, when Judson saw men enslaved by the chains of sin and self, he was able to proclaim the message of freedom in Christ with a conviction that previously had not been present in his preaching. He was not talking theory now, nor was he parroting pleasant platitudes. He was talking with the fervor of one who had been in prison, one who knew what it is to be a captive in chains, one who could relate the experiences of that captivity to the bondage of those imprisoned by sin.

In each instance, though the letter of his prayer was denied, the spirit of his prayer was honored. The prayer behind his prayer was answered. Thus he could say near the close of his days: "I never prayed sincerely or earnestly for anything but that it came at sometime . . . in some shape." He knew that "no" can really mean "yes" when God wants to serve some larger purpose than the person who prays could understand.

Or come a step closer to the inner circle of the saints. Ponder the story of Moses, who repeatedly prayed he might enter into the Promised Land, but whose petition was not granted.

Here was a giant among men, a stalwart of the Lord, a leader of the people. Yet the one thing for which he repeatedly prayed was denied him. Why? Because this man who stood for God in the midst of the people had on one occasion been exceedingly ungodly. In a moment of anger and impatience he had smitten a rock in disobedience to God. The false image of God which that act gave to an immature people had to be erased. Somehow they needed to know that this picture of God as one with flashing eyes and flailing fist was distorted. More important, they needed to learn that no man — even a leader — can sin and get away with it.

Moses had dishonored God. For the sake of the people, more than his own, he had to be punished. So, God, in effect, said to him: "Moses, you will not go into Canaan. You may lead the people up to the border. You may even see inside. But you cannot go in."

How Moses prayed for a reprieve! How he earnestly petitioned God for a reversal of this decision. Not once, but over and over he asked until God finally said:

Speak no more to me of this matter.
Deuteronomy 3:26

I believe that if only Moses had been involved, God would have granted his request. God loved him. But there were the people to be considered. They had to be taught the necessity of obedience, and in a way they would never forget. So his petition was denied in order that this larger purpose might be served. Ever since then, Hebrew and Christian mothers have taken their children into their arms and have told their little ones, who always love a story, about Moses — a man of God, a leader of the people, a stalwart of the faith — who could not go into the Promised Land because he was disobedient. Through the telling of that tale, both young and old have had this great fact nailed down for them: Disobedience can be forgiven, but the consequences must still be faced.

If Moses could speak to us now, I believe he would say he is glad his prayer was denied. Deeper, wider, and higher than any concern for personal achievement was Moses' desire to lead the people into full possession of all God had promised them. This was the prayer behind his prayer. When his superficial desire was denied, his real request was answered. He was given a "no" which turned out to be "yes," and thus a larger purpose was served.

Or consider the experience of Paul. Three times Paul prayed that he might be relieved from a "thorn in the flesh." So far as we know, he never was. He carried this malady (eye trouble, epilepsy, allergy, recurrent attacks of malaria?) with him to the grave. But did Paul pray in vain? Not at all. Though God denied the petition, he answered the man. He said to Paul:

My grace is sufficient for you.
2 Corinthians 12:9

Through this grace of God, Paul learned to triumph in suffering. He entered into a relationship with the Father such as few men have shared. With the pain came the presence of Jesus and the persuasion that:

The sufferings of this present time are not worth comparing with the glory that is to be revealed to us. Romans 8:18

For Paul that gift was quite enough. Although his petition (that he might be relieved from the thorn in the flesh) was denied, the petition behind his petition, the longing behind his longing, the desire behind his desire (to know Jesus and the power of his resurrection) was granted. And Paul lived to speak lovingly of the day when "no" was really "yes."

One last scene completes the picture, and here we truly tread on holy ground. A figure kneels in the Garden of Gethsemane. Below him is the brook of Kidron. Behind him stands a grove of gnarled olive trees. Above him is a rotund moon whose brightness makes the shadowy rocks all the more foreboding. As he kneels there, this One who knew no sin struggles with the indescribable horror of taking on himself the sin of the world:

My Father, if it be possible, let this cup pass from me. Matthew 26:39

There is desperate urgency in these words. "If there is any other way—if there is any other alternative—if there is any other means whereby the salvation of the world can be secured, let this cup pass."

But the cup did not pass. Why not? So the prayer behind his prayer (that all might be saved) could be answered. Through a momentary denial of the letter of Jesus' prayer, there came the eternal answer to the spirit of his prayer. The real purpose for which he had come was fulfilled. Thus, in the most wonderfully significant way ever known, God's "no" became "yes."

Do you see now the wonder and wisdom of

the third floor in God's house of prayer? By a delayed or disguised answer he is able to serve some larger purpose or to teach the wisdom of his way. Or perhaps even to provide you with more than you ask for. Do not try to limit God as to the method of his reply. Do not confine him to only one answer. Instead, seek to know and do his will more fully, persuaded that what he plans for you is better than anything you plan for yourself.

Perhaps this reasoning can help you to see more clearly the "yes" behind the "no" that sometimes greets your prayers for a Christian loved one who is close to death. If you have followed the biblical injunction, you have prayed for the healing light and love of Jesus to bring help and hope and wholeness. But, having prayed the prayer of faith, you must not limit God to a temporary restoration of the flesh. Remember that from the Christian point of view, which measures things not by time but by eternity, death may be the only true healing there is. Certainly it is the only complete healing, the ultimate instance in which "no" is really "yes."

A mother who had prayed earnestly that her boy might return from the war unscathed found herself clutching a telegram which began with the harrowing words: "We regret to inform you. . . ." For a while her faith was shattered. But later God gave her grace to write these words:

We asked that he might live: Eternal Love
From out the fulness of His boundless store

Hath granted him to share the life above,
Alive for evermore.

We asked for health: and faith can almost see
His radiant face, his movements swift and strong:
With every power quickened, joyously
His soul is breathing song.

We prayed at last, that he again might come
To see the home that he had held so dear:
And peacefully he reached a fairer Home,
And dearer — but not here.

O Wisdom infinite and Love supreme!
This light on sorrow, care and doubt is thrown,
Beyond our prayers, our hopes, our brightest dream,
What God hath given His own.[2]

CORRECTIVES

For Ailment Ten
Misreading God's Kindness. Before closing the ledger and marking a prayer "unanswered," check to see whether, in kindness, God has not given more than you bargained for. He often ignores what you say and responds to what you mean. Let him!

For Ailment Eleven
Misunderstanding God's Way. God's way is best. Despite seeming proof to the contrary, a search for the more enduring evidence demonstrates this

principle to be true. The apparent denial is often God working in "mysterious ways his wonders to perform."

For Ailment Twelve
Miscalculating God's Purpose. The letter and the spirit of your prayer are not always the same. Therefore, God's greater interest is in the prayer behind your prayer, the desire behind your desire. He wants to serve this larger purpose. So do not limit him as to the method of his reply. Do not confine him to only one answer. A delayed or disguised response may be his way of giving what you have been seeking all along.

FIVE
The Answer God Gives

Having suggested twelve reasons why prayers are unanswered, I must now add what you may have already surmised: No true prayer is ever unanswered. The foregoing information has been given to point out obstacles to effective prayer, which keep God from doing what he really wants to do. He *wants* to "give you the desires of your heart." True prayer is communion with God. It is being in his holy presence. It is sharing heart-to-heart fellowship with the heavenly Father. And this experience is self-rewarding, even as being in the presence of evil is self-defeating.

One day I was invited to address a convention of businessmen in Los Angeles. For several weeks a crowded calendar had denied me the joy of being with my son (who was ten at the time). Anxious to "play catch up," I invited him to go along. We had a good visit while driving down. During the dinner hour he met some interesting

people who added to his enjoyment. I told a few
jokes as part of my speech which made that
easier to take. All in all we had a great time. As
we started home over the famed Grapevine Pass
I suggested, "Jeff, why don't you curl up here on
the seat and go to sleep?"

"No, sir!" he replied. "For nearly five hours
I've had you all to myself and I want this to last
as long as it can."

I knew there was something special about
those hours which made them precious to me. It
took my boy to phrase it. They had been rich
because we shared a rare experience of togetherness.
We had really given ourselves to each other.

In true prayer a similar sense of oneness can
develop between you and God. You can have
him all to yourself. You can be alone with him.
You can share an experience of fellowship with
the heavenly Father, and this will provide its
own reward.

EXCLUSIVELY YOURS

Does such intimacy with God seem impossible?
Do you stumble, as I did at one time, over the
thought of having God all to yourself? Does it
worry you that in having his undivided attention
you might be keeping him from someone else
who needs him more? I used to feel that way. In
fact, my sense of sub-Christian guilt often kept
me from praying at all. I didn't want to trouble
him. I felt he was too busy to bother with the
likes of me. My problem was twofold: First, a
feeling of false humility which led me to feel
unworthy of his attention (but no son of God

should ever grovel, for he is a child of the King!), and, second, an infantile image of God which kept him bound up in the stream of time. I pictured God as an overtaxed switchboard operator trying valiantly to answer the millions of prayers which were coming to him all at one time from various parts of the earth. I could see him sitting somewhere trying frantically to plug in the right answer to the right petition, but never quite making it. From time to time the connections got crossed, and then it rained when the sun should have shone. Or someone died when he should have gotten better. I had God locked up in time; I had him living in my stream of consciousness. But I was wrong. He isn't limited in that way at all. His life isn't measured, as ours is, by a clock or a calendar. For God there is no past or future; there is only an eternal now.

In his gem of a book *Beyond Personality*, C.S. Lewis makes this fact wonderfully clear.

> If a million people were praying to Him at ten-thirty tonight, He hasn't got to listen to them all in that little snippet which we call ten-thirty. Ten-thirty—and every other moment from the beginning of the world—is always the Present for Him. If you like to put it that way, He has all eternity to listen to the split-second prayer put up by a pilot as his plane crashes in flames.[3]

Or, to understand it another way, also suggested by Lewis, here is a man writing a book.

One of his characters is called Mary. In the course of the novel he writes: "Just then the telephone rang. Mary laid down the book she was reading and picked up the receiver."

Now for Mary, who lives in the imaginary time of the author's novel, there is no delay between the moment the telephone rang and the moment she laid down the book and picked up the receiver. But for the author, the man who is Mary's creator, this is not so. He does not live in that imaginary time at all. And, between the writings of the first half of that sentence— "Just then the telephone rang"—and the second half— "Mary laid down the book she was reading and picked up the receiver"—he might sit for three or four hours and think steadily about Mary.

In fact, he could think about her as if she were the only character in his book. He could do so as long as he pleased. And this is the important part: *The hours he spent in thinking about her and being exclusively concerned about her would not appear in her time, the imaginary time of the novel, at all.*

This is just an illustration, and any illustration can be pushed too far. But perhaps it gives you a small glimpse of the truth about God. Lewis continues:

> God is not hurried along in the Time-stream of this universe any more than an author is hurried along in the imaginary time of his own novel. He has infinite attention to spare for each one of us. He doesn't have to

deal with us in the mass. You are as much alone with Him as if you were the only being He had ever created.[4]

True prayer is always answered by the very fact of gaining an audience with God. Your visit with the heavenly Father is in itself an answer. And furthermore, this bears its own reward, for God gives you himself.

THE DESIRE OF YOUR HEART

In the Thirty-seventh Psalm there is a verse which brings this thrilling thought into sharper focus:

Take delight in the Lord, and he will give you the desires of your heart. Psalm 37:4

Some people after reading that verse have concluded: "If I tip my hat to the heavenly Father, he in turn will give me the multitude of things I want." But they are mistaken. What it really says is this: If you delight yourself in God — that is, if you make him the central object of your attention and affection so that he becomes the desire of your heart — he in turn will give you that desire. He will give you himself. What a tremendous thought!

In true prayer this experience always happens. You make a pilgrimage into the presence of the heavenly Father and discover he is all you need, and more besides. He is life, health, wisdom, power, truth, love . . . the list goes on and on. When he gives you himself, he gives you these attributes of himself. You are made whole. Why? Because you have *him*.

If this tremendous truth gets hold of you, it will revolutionize your thoughts about prayer. Instead of the dull ordeal it has often been, prayer will become the sheer delight you want it to be. The concerns with which you have often come to God (as if they were matters of life and death) will find their proper level as you experience the joy of being with him.

A young Harvard student secured an appointment with Dr. Phillips Brooks to discuss a perplexing problem. He wanted the great preacher's guidance. After an hour alone with the good doctor he returned to the dormitory where one of his friends asked, "What did the preacher say? Did he help you with your problem?"

"Do you know something?" the student responded, a note of wonder in his voice. "I forgot to mention it. It just didn't seem important when I began talking with Phillips Brooks." Then, he added softly, "I can tell you this, though: It doesn't seem insurmountable any more." The contagion of a radiant and victorious personality lifted the boy above his problem. From that nobler perspective he could see things more clearly. He knew that with God's help all things are possible.

In a far more satisfying way this joy can happen to you when in true prayer you enter the presence of God. So great will be the glory of being with him, so satisfying will be the knowledge that in having him you have all you need, so energizing will be the infusion of his power, that your previously insurmountable problem just won't matter. You will return from this divine appointment with a calm assurance that through Christ you are more than conqueror. True prayer is always answered, for true prayer is communion with God. And such communion is self-rewarding.

There is, as you know, a form of communication above and beyond words. A relationship "so intimate that thoughts and feelings pass from soul to soul" without a word being said. A young lady was expecting a visit from her fiance who had been away at school. There was so much to talk about that she wondered how one evening could possibly suffice. When a friend met her the following morning and inquired how things had gone, the girl replied, "Do you know what we did last night? We just sat for two hours—*two hours*—and never said a word!" So sweet had been the communion between them, their hearts understood each other without resorting to words.

When you enter into true prayer, you share a similar experience. You enjoy such a satisfying sense of God's presence that the details of your visit are obscured by the joy of being with him. Though no words pass between you and God, your prayer is answered as he who has become the desire of your heart, gives you himself.

KEEP ON KEEPING ON

Obviously, this kind of glory is not easily won. It does not come at the first attempt. You must not become discouraged if your first stumbling efforts in prayer do not take you to the summit. A person who has just begun climbing mountains does not grow discouraged if he fails to top Everest on first try. There are lesser peaks upon which he can practice as he prepares himself for the steeper climb. In prayer you must be willing to attempt the foothills before you try for the mountaintop. But you should always keep the mountaintop in sight! Your goal is true prayer. That is, nothing less than a sense of the presence of God. So keep on keeping on.

Diamonds are rarely found on the surface of the ground. They generally are the product of much mining. Similarly, the jewels of the spirit are rarely stumbled on. The surface soil of attention-getting things must be cleared away. The gravel of your own resistance and the hard rock of your own rebellion must be burrowed through. But finally, by keeping on, you are rewarded with that jewel of great price—God's grandest gift—himself. True prayer is always answered, for true prayer is communion with God. And this is self-rewarding.

"NO" IS AN ANSWER TOO

But what about the petitions you bring with you? Does God always grant these? The answer is "no," for one or more of the twelve reasons I have already discussed. True, he does answer many prayers in the affirmative. Instances of this are far too numerous to be ignored. God says "yes" many times. Not only by giving you himself, but by granting your lesser petitions.

But what about those times when instead of "yes," his answer is "no"? Then you must remember that "no" is an answer too. In fact, there are times when "no" is the only answer which love and wisdom can give. For God to answer "yes" would be to harm or hamper you. So when you pray, seek for maturity enough to know there may be victory in defeat and profit in prayers denied.

Personally, I have lived long enough to thank God that some of my prayers were not answered in the affirmative. Through the 20-20 vision with which hindsight is equipped, I have come to see that "no" was a far better answer in some instances than "yes." You may be able to say the same. So, while you continue to come to God with your supplications, never hesitating to ask him for those things which you deem desirable, remember he will not give you everything you ask for—not because he is stingy but because he is wise, not because he is indifferent but because he really cares about you.

When still a youngster, my son would often start a conversation by saying, "Dad, I know you're going to say 'no,' but . . ." and then he would reel off some natural or spontaneous request. Occasionally, to his surprise, his request was granted. More often, his prejudgment of the situation was correct, and my answer was "no." Then, believe it or not, he was relieved. My denial had served to confirm and strengthen his own evaluation of the situation. He usually knew before he asked, which request was unwise, but he found himself in tension. There was a conflict between what he wanted and what he knew was best. My denial helped him to resolve the conflict and reassured him his best judgment was correct. Through a repetition of this process he, in time and by the grace of God, learned to weigh all the alternatives with which life confronts him and, for the most part, comes to right conclusions on his own.

If I had been so weak and unwise as to grant my son every whim and fancy that came to mind, I would have done him a grave disservice. I would have spoiled him in a way far more devastating than the word normally implies. I would have failed to provide the necessary confirmation of his own correct opinions which he needed to develop the essential self-reliance necessary in adulthood. "No" is an answer as well as "yes," and sometimes it is the only answer which God, in his love and wisdom, can give to his children.

> I will not doubt, though all my ships at sea
>   Come drifting home with broken masts and sails;
> I shall believe the Hand which never fails,
> From seeming evil worketh good to me;
>   And, though I weep because those sails are battered,
>   Still will I cry, while my best hopes lie shattered,
>   "I trust in Thee."
>
> I will not doubt, though all my prayers return
>   Unanswered from the still, white realm above;

I shall believe it is an all-wise Love
Which has refused those things for which I
   yearn;
   And though, at times, I cannot keep from
      grieving,
   Yet the pure ardor of my fixed believing
      Undimmed shall burn.

                              Ella Wheeler Wilcox[5]

THE GRACE OF WAITING

One more thought completes the picture. Sometimes neither "yes" nor "no" is the right answer. In these cases, the answer God gives is, "Wait a while."

Waiting is not one of the arts for which our generation is famous, but it is a virtue we all must learn if we wish to make effective use of prayer. In prayer you are dealing with One to whom

> *A thousand years . . . are but as yesterday when it is past, or as a watch in the night.* Psalm 90:4

God's grandest gifts are often gained only by waiting. The old tales of the sea illustrate this truth. There were the little ships which sailed the coastal waters and carried the ordinary things of life from port to port. They were important, because without them the routine needs of daily life could not be met. But it was the great Spanish galleons which put out to sea for extended journeys into unknown waters that came home with richer freight.

Similarly, the little barks of prayer which you put out day by day bring you the small necessities of life, though they never venture far from shore. But it is the great prayers, like the mighty sailing ships of old, which mount the winds of faith and are borne to some farther shore, which reap the rich rewards. They are not so quick to return as the smaller craft. Often there is much anguish in waiting, but it is worth your while, for when they come their holds are filled with golden treasures.

Therefore the Lord waits to be gracious to you. Isaiah 30:18

So when your prayers are not answered in the precise time or fashion which you fancy best, wait on the Lord. God does not measure things as you do. He has eternity's values in view. And in his good time the ship of prayer you may have thought lost at sea will come sailing into port bearing blessings which only a long journey into faith and the grace of waiting can win.

God answers prayer; sometimes when hearts are weak
He gives the very gifts believers seek.
But often faith must learn a deeper rest,
And trust God's silence when He does not speak;
For He whose name is Love will send the best.
Stars may burn out, nor mountain walls endure,
But God is true, His promises are sure
   For those who seek.

Myra Goodwin Plantz

NOTES

1. Based on an article "The Heart of Prayer," by Norman Vincent Peale in *Guideposts*, June 1958.

2. Quoted in Robert J. McCracken's "A Sermon for Those Who Are Tempted to Give Up Praying," printed in pamphlet form by The Riverside Church, New York City.

3. C.S. Lewis, *Beyond Personality* (New York: The Macmillan Company, 1948), p. 15.

4. *Ibid.*, p. 16.

5. Ella Wheeler Wilcox, "Faith." Used by permission of Rand McNally & Co.